DELICIOUS PASTA DISHES

CONTENTS

FAST PASTA AND NOODLE DISHES

Pasta and noodle dishes are always a treat and can be prepared quickly and easily. What's more, this special food is infinitely variable. From all over the world, we have collected an assortment of delicious sauces and a vast array of pastas—spaghetti, penne, tagliatelle, rice noodles, and more.

NORTH AMERICA & AUSTRALIA

Immigrants from Italy and China brought many rich culinary traditions to their new homelands. While continuing to make their favorite dishes, they often worked with local ingredients, such as sun-ripened vegetables from California. In this way, original combinations as well as classics with delicious new twists—like creamy spaghetti "tetrazzini" with chicken, pappardelle, and ham—made their debuts.

Without a doubt, pasta is most often associated with Italy, even if it did originate in China! Italian chefs and home cooks created simple yet exquisite dishes that combined pasta with typically Mediterranean ingre-

NORTHERN AND EASTERN EUROPE

Noodle dishes from this region are hearty and warming. Pasta dough is often prepared at home, then either rolled and stuffed with a savory filling, baked in a casserole, or tossed with a delectable sauce. Bacon, sausage, and cheese are favorite ingredients in many rib-sticking yet refined dishes.

ASIA AND THE FAR EAST

Along with rice, noodles are one of the main food staples of these lands. Exotic ingredients like Chinese five-spice powder, oyster sauce, and shiitake mushrooms lend Asian and Far Eastern noodle dishes their special appeal. These delicacies are fragrant, flavorful, and beautifully presented—and most of them are easy to make in the miraculously quick-cooking wok!

dients. Aromatic vegetables and herbs, fresh seafood, delicious wild mushrooms, and zesty cheeses of Mediterranean origin are now widely available, giving pasta specialties the distinctive flavor all can enjoy.

FETTUCCINE IN A CREAMY CHEESE SAUCE

This warming dish is sure to please both family and friends. Two cheeses flavor the rich, mild sauce, which is the perfect topping for ribbony fettuccine noodles.

INGREDIENTS
(Serves 4)

- 4 tablespoons butter
- 6 tablespoons flour
- 2 cups milk
- salt and white pepper
- pinch of grated nutmeg
- 1 pound fettuccine
- 1 egg yolk
- ½ cup heavy cream
- ½ cup grated Parmesan
- ½ cup shredded fontina or Swiss cheese

INGREDIENT TIPS

- For a more pungent cheese sauce, substitute pecorino for Parmesan and Gruyère for fontina.
- You can also vary the flavor of the sauce by adding a splash of tangy lemon juice or dry champagne.

1 Melt the butter in a large saucepan over medium heat. Add the flour; cook, stirring, for 3 minutes, until bubbly, not brown.

2 Slowly add the milk, stirring constantly. Add ¼ teaspoon salt, ¼ teaspoon pepper, and the nutmeg. Simmer over low heat until thickened, 8–10 minutes.

3 In a large saucepan of boiling salted water, cook the fettuccine according to the directions on the package until al dente.

4 Meanwhile, in a small bowl, mix the egg yolk with the cream. Remove the sauce from the heat. Gradually stir one third of the hot sauce into the yolk mixture, then add the mixture back into the sauce in the pan, stirring constantly. Heat the sauce for 2 minutes without boiling so the egg yolk will not curdle. Pour the sauce through a fine sieve into a large saucepan. Add the cheeses and stir until melted. Keep warm over low heat, and do not boil.

5 Drain the pasta well, add to the sauce, and gently toss to coat. Place in a deep serving platter and serve in pasta bowls.

Step 1

Step 4

Step 4

Preparation: 10 minutes
Cooking: 20 minutes
Per serving: 859 cal; 29 g pro; 37 g fat; 101 g carb.

TYPICALLY VALLE D'AOSTA
One of the most famous cheeses from this rugged, picturesque Alpine region of Italy is fontina. It's perfect for cooking because it melts easily and has a light, mildly sweet taste that pleasantly underscores the flavors of accompanying ingredients.

COOKING TIP

Try this recipe with fresh noodles, which you can find in the refrigerated section of your supermarket. If you can find colorful noodles, try them here—they will look beautiful, and the ingredients that give them their color (spinach, tomato, etc.) will lend the dish a flavorful accent.

SERVING TIPS

Garnish the finished noodles with fresh herbs and serve Italian bread on the side for dipping in the sauce.

 Enjoy a glass of crisp Italian white wine, like an Orvieto, or sparkling mineral water.

TAGLIERINI WITH BOLOGNESE SAUCE

ITALY

Bolognese sauce is a high point of Italian cuisine. In Italy it most often accompanies long, flat strands of pasta, such as tagliatelle or taglierini.

INGREDIENTS

(Serves 8)

- 2 carrots
- 1 onion
- 1 garlic clove
- 2 celery ribs
- 1 pound plum tomatoes
- 1 can (28 ounces) peeled whole tomatoes
- ¼ pound sliced prosciutto
- 1 tablespoon oil
- ½ cup chopped parsley
- ¾ pound ground beef or veal
- 3 tablespoons tomato paste
- I cup beef broth
- salt and pepper
- 1 pound *each* spinach and plain taglierini or linguini
- 4 tablespoons butter
- ½ cup grated Parmesan

INGREDIENT TIP

Instead of plum tomatoes, you can use canned peeled whole tomatoes, drained.

1 Peel and chop the carrots, onion, and garlic. Chop the celery, plum tomatoes, and prosciutto. Then drain and chop the canned tomatoes.

2 Heat the oil in a large skillet over medium-high heat. Sauté the carrots, onion, garlic and celery for 3 minutes, until the onions are translucent. Add the parsley and sauté for 1 minute.

3 Add the beef and sauté for 5 minutes, until browned. Add the prosciutto and sauté for 5 minutes. Add the tomato paste and cook for 1 minute. Add the broth, canned tomatoes, 1¼ teaspoons salt, and ½ teaspoon pepper. Mix well and bring to a boil. Simmer over medium heat, partially covered, for 45 minutes, stirring occasionally.

4 When the sauce is almost ready, cook both varieties of taglierini together in a large saucepan of boiling salted water according to the directions on the package until al dente. Drain the pasta.

5 Stir the butter into the sauce. Place the sauce and pasta on plates, and sprinkle with grated Parmesan.

Step 1

Step 1

Step 3

Preparation: 15 minutes
Cooking: 1 hour
Per serving: 734 cal; 30 g pro; 25 g fat; 98 g carb.

TYPICALLY BOLOGNESE

Bologna is the capital of the Emilia-Romagna region of Italy and the birthplace of this world-famous meat sauce. To this day, the true origins of the recipe—as well as the acceptable variations—are subjects of heated debate among passionate, food-loving Italians.

Cooking Tip

Italians often vary their much-loved Bolognese sauce, replacing a part of the mixed ground beef with ground lamb or rabbit. Some things, however, always remain the same—the quality and freshness of the ingredients, and the slow stewing of the meat.

Serving Tips

A tasty appetizer is a red, white, and green salad of tomato, fresh mozzarella, and basil leaves.

🍷 Serve a hearty Italian red wine, such as a Barolo or Barbaresco.

$\mathscr{S}$UMPTUOUS SALMON TAGLIATELLE

ITALY

Seafood lovers will adore this Italian favorite. Long, tender tagliatelle noodles make an ideal base for the creamy sauce, which gains rich flavor and texture from bits of flaky salmon.

INGREDIENTS
(Serves 6)

- 1 onion
- 3 tablespoons butter
- ½ cup dry white wine
- 1½ cups heavy cream
- 1 pound tagliatelle
- ¾ pound salmon fillets (skinless)
- salt and pepper
- juice of ½ lime or lemon
- fresh basil leaves

INGREDIENT TIP

If you want to make this a vegetarian main dish, omit the salmon and simply stir ½ pound of blanched diced vegetables or frozen peas into the sauce.

1 Peel and finely chop the onion. In a large saucepan over medium-high heat, melt 1 tablespoon butter and sauté the onion for 2 minutes, until translucent. Add the wine, bring to a boil, and cook until the wine is reduced by half, about 5 minutes. Reduce the heat to medium, add the cream, and heat to boiling. Simmer until the liquid is reduced by half, about 5 minutes.

Step 1

2 Meanwhile, cook the tagliatelle in a large pot of boiling salted water according to the directions on the package until al dente.

3 Cut the salmon into ½-inch cubes. Add the remaining butter, ½ teaspoon salt, ¼ teaspoon pepper, and the lime juice to the sauce and puree using a hand blender or a whisk.

Step 3

4 Add the salmon to the sauce. Simmer over medium-low heat for 3 minutes. Remove the pan from the heat. Drain the pasta and place in shallow bowls. Pour the sauce over the pasta and garnish with the basil leaves.

Step 4

Preparation: 15 minutes
Cooking: 15 minutes
Per serving: 666 cal; 23 g pro; 35 g fat; 61 g carb.

TYPICALLY ITALIAN
Italian menus almost invariably include seafood, which restaurant chefs and home cooks purchase fresh at local fish markets. Boot-shaped Italy has an extensive coastline and is perfectly situated to enjoy the rich harvest of the Mediterranean Sea.

COOKING TIP

Ribbon pastas—tagliatelle, fettuccine, or the especially wide pappardelle—are perfectly suited to this recipe, as the creamy sauce and chunks of fish cling to the noodles.

SERVING TIPS

As an appetizer, try serving an *insalata di funghi*, a mushroom salad that you can prepare with a zesty herb vinaigrette.

 To accompany this dish, look for a sparkling dry Prosecco or Asti Spumante.

SERVING TIPS Serve the ravioli as a main course, after a colorful vegetable soup to start.

As a suitable accompaniment, enjoy a fresh fruity white wine, champagne, or a crisp cider.

RAVIOLI WITH ZESTY CREAM SAUCE

ITALY

With ready-made pasta, you can prepare a quick yet memorable dish in a matter of minutes. Here, an easy-to-make herb sauce turns fresh ravioli into a unique pleasure.

INGREDIENTS
(Serves 6)

- 2 pounds meat or cheese ravioli
- 1 small onion
- 1 garlic clove
- 1½ tablespoons butter
- 1½ tablespoons flour
- 1 cup milk
- 1 cup heavy cream
- ½ cup white wine
- 2 tablespoons chopped fresh basil or tarragon
- 1 teaspoon lemon juice
- salt and white pepper
- pinch of cayenne pepper

INGREDIENT TIPS

- Depending on the ravioli filling and the season, you might replace the basil with parsley, chives, or thyme.
- For a richer alternative, melt ½ cup gorgonzola cheese into the sauce.

1 In a large saucepan of boiling salted water, cook the ravioli according to the package directions until they rise to the surface. While the ravioli cooks, peel and finely chop the onion and garlic.

2 Melt the butter in a small saucepan over medium-high heat, and sauté the onion and garlic until the onion is translucent, 2–3 minutes. Stir in the flour, then the milk, cream, and wine. Bring to a boil, then simmer over low heat for 5 minutes, until slightly thickened.

3 Stir the basil, lemon juice, ½ teaspoon salt, ¼ teaspoon white pepper, and the cayenne into the sauce.

4 Drain the cooked ravioli and divide among warmed plates. Pour the sauce on top and serve immediately.

Step 1

Step 2

Step 3

Preparation: 10 minutes
Cooking: 20 minutes
Per serving: 667 cal; 25 g pro;
39 g fat; 52 g carb.

TYPICALLY LIGURIAN
The coast of the Northern Italian region of Liguria is steep and rugged, making it difficult to raise livestock. This fact also shapes Ligurian cuisine, which is often vegetarian and above all characterized by a preference for fresh herbs.

ℋERBED MUSHROOM PAPPARDELLE

ITALY

Here's a delightful sauce that takes very little time to make. Broad ribbon noodles serve as a perfect foundation for the delicate mushrooms, juicy tomatoes, and fresh aromatic herbs.

INGREDIENTS
(Serves 4)

- 1 pound fresh porcini, cremini or white mushrooms
- 1 onion
- 1 garlic clove
- 1 large celery rib
- 1 pound tomatoes
- 1 pound pappardelle
- 1 sprig fresh thyme
- a few leaves of fresh basil and parsley
- ¼ cup olive oil
- salt and pepper
- 2 tablespoons butter
- freshly grated Parmesan

INGREDIENT TIP

This recipe calls for an equal amount of mushrooms and noodles. Try the dish with other kinds of mushrooms—chanterelles, for example. If you can't find any wild forest mushrooms, just use fresh white button mushrooms.

1 Wipe the mushrooms with a damp paper towel. Peel the stems and slice the mushrooms lengthwise. Peel and dice the onion and garlic. Wash and dice the celery.

2 In a large saucepan of boiling water, blanch the tomatoes. Add salt to the water and cook the pasta according to the directions on the package until al dente.

3 Peel the tomatoes, cut into quarters, remove the stems and seeds and finely cube the flesh. Coarsely chop the herbs.

4 Heat the oil in a large skillet and sauté the onion and garlic over medium-high heat until the onion is transparent, about 5 minutes. Add the celery and sauté for 2 minutes. Over high heat, add the mushrooms and sauté for 5 minutes. Add the tomatoes, herbs, 1½ teaspoons salt and ½ teaspoon pepper; sauté for 2 minutes.

5 Drain the pasta in a colander and place in a large bowl. Add the butter and toss until the butter melts and coats the pasta. Divide the pasta among 4 shallow bowls, top with sauce and sprinkle with Parmesan.

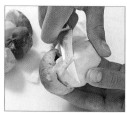

Step 1

Step 4

Step 5

Preparation: 25 minutes
Cooking: 20 minutes
Per serving: 662 cal, 19 g pro,
22 g fat, 100 g carb.

TYPICALLY PIEDMONTESE
When the morning fog hangs over the forests of Piedmont in spring and fall, it's mushroom season—time for the exclusive and coveted porcini to be gathered. Thanks to their firm consistency, porcini are easily transported and arrive at market in good condition.

COOKING TIP

There's no need to use two pans of boiling water (one for blanching the tomatoes and the other for cooking the pasta). Simply blanch the tomatoes first, remove them from the pan with a slotted spoon, then add salt and the pasta to the boiling water.

SERVING TIPS

Follow this delicious dish with vanilla ice cream or lemon sorbet, generously sprinkled with fresh blueberries.

A strong red wine from the Piedmont region, such as a Barbaresco, complements the meal.

SERVING TIPS This pasta makes a hearty main course but is also a great side dish with grilled steaks.

With this dish, offer a refreshing white wine, such as a Frascati, or a light red wine.

PENNE ALL'ARRABBIATA

ITALY

All'arrabbiata, *which means "angry" in Italian, refers to the fiery temper of this dish. A few perfectly combined ingredients make up its simple, lively composition.*

INGREDIENTS
(Serves 4)

- ¼ pound bacon
- 1 pound tomatoes or 1 can (28 ounces) peeled whole tomatoes
- salt and black pepper
- 1 pound penne
- 1 onion
- 2 garlic cloves
- 2 red chiles (Thai bird) or ½ teaspoon crushed red pepper
- 1 tablespoon olive oil
- 1 cup tightly packed Italian parsley leaves
- grated Parmesan or pecorino cheese

INGREDIENT TIP

Try pancetta, an Italian bacon that's generally less salty than the American kind. You'll find it in Italian grocery stores.

1 Finely chop the bacon. In a large saucepan of boiling water, blanch the tomatoes (if using fresh). Peel, cube, and press through a sieve set over a bowl.

2 Add salt to the water used to blanch the tomatoes, then add the penne. Cook according to the directions on the package until al dente.

3 Meanwhile, peel and chop the onion and garlic. Cut the chiles in half lengthwise, remove the seeds and membranes, and finely chop.

4 Heat the oil in a large saucepan over medium heat. Add the bacon and sauté for 2 minutes. Add the onion, garlic, chiles, ½ teaspoon salt, and ¼ teaspoon black pepper, and sauté until the onion is translucent, about 5 minutes. Add the tomatoes, heat to boiling, and simmer for 8 minutes. Finely chop the parsley.

5 Drain the pasta and add to the sauce. Add the parsley and toss until well mixed. Serve the cheese on the side.

Step 1

Step 3

Step 5

Preparation: 15 minutes
Cooking: 20 minutes
Per serving: 664 cal; 19 g pro; 22 g fat; 97 g carb.

TYPICALLY LAZIO

Lazio, the region of Italy just south of Tuscany and Umbria, includes rural areas as well as cosmopolitan Rome. The cuisine reflects this contrast—simple, very fresh ingredients are combined into delicious dishes that have worldwide appeal.

LINGUINE WITH RICOTTA AND HERBS

ITALY

Here's a light, fragrant dish you can prepare in a flash. Juicy, sweet cherry tomatoes, creamy ricotta cheese, and fresh green herbs flavor this vibrant, colorful sauce.

INGREDIENTS
(Serves 4)

- 1 onion
- 1 pint cherry tomatoes
- 6 tablespoons olive oil
- ¼ cup chopped mixed herbs (for example, parsley, sage, thyme, rosemary, tarragon, or basil)
- salt and white pepper
- 1 pound linguine
- 1 cup ricotta cheese

INGREDIENT TIP

If you can't find ricotta, you can use another firm, fresh cheese, such as cottage or farmer cheese.

1 Peel and dice the onion. Quarter each of the tomatoes. Heat the oil in a large saucepan over medium-high heat. Add the onion to the pan and cook until translucent, about 5 minutes.

2 Add the tomatoes, herbs, 1½ teaspoons salt and ½ teaspoon white pepper. Simmer over low heat until a thick sauce forms, about 5 minutes.

3 Meanwhile, in a large pot of boiling salted water, cook the pasta according to the directions on the package until al dente.

4 Drain the pasta in a colander, reserving about ½ cup cooking water. Add the pasta to the sauce and toss to mix. Remove the pan from the heat, add the ricotta and mix well. If necessary, thin the ricotta and sauce with the pasta cooking water. Serve in warmed shallow bowls.

Step 1

Step 2

Step 4

Preparation: 25 minutes
Cooking: 10 minutes
Per serving: 736 cal; 22 g pro;
30 g fat; 93 g carb.

TYPICALLY ITALIAN
Ricotta, a fresh and creamy Italian cheese, is made from the whey of sheep, water buffalo, and occasionally goat or cow's milk. (Most ricotta available in the United States is made from cow's milk.)

COOKING TIPS

• Remove the pan from the heat before adding the ricotta so that the cheese remains creamy.

• Leftovers can be warmed up without losing any of their fine flavor. Or if you like, keep the dish cool—add a splash of lemon juice or vinegar, then toss and serve as a pasta salad.

SERVING TIPS

Offer bread and *insalata mista,* a salad of mixed greens, as an appetizer or alongside the main course.

🍷 Fruity white wine or Prosecco, a light sparkling white wine, rounds off this delicate meal.

CREAMY TAGLIATELLE AND SPINACH

ITALY

This scrumptious vegetarian sauce features tender spinach and rich fresh cream. Just before tossing with the pasta, a splash of lemon juice is added for a flavor boost.

INGREDIENTS
(Serves 4)

- 1 pound fresh spinach
- 1 onion
- 1 garlic clove
- 1 pound tagliatelle
- 2 tablespoons butter
- 1 cup heavy cream
- salt and white pepper
- pinch of grated nutmeg
- ¼ cup grated Parmesan
- 1 tablespoon lemon juice

INGREDIENT TIP
Ideally, this dish should be made with tender spring spinach, which has light green leaves and a mild taste. But in winter or late summer, it's fine to use the somewhat heartier, spicier winter spinach or frozen leaf spinach.

1 Clean the spinach, cutting off the thick stems and discarding the yellow leaves. Rinse the spinach several times in cold water until there is no trace of sand in the basin. Spin dry. Peel and dice the onion and garlic.

2 Cook the pasta in a large saucepan of boiling salted water according to the directions on the package until al dente.

3 Meanwhile, melt the butter in a large heavy saucepan over medium-high heat, and sauté the onion and garlic until the onion is translucent, about 5 minutes. Add the spinach and cook until the leaves wilt.

4 Stir in the cream, ½ teaspoon salt, ½ teaspoon white pepper and the nutmeg. Heat to boiling. Stir in the Parmesan.

5 Drain the pasta, reserving about ½ cup cooking water. Remove the sauce from the heat. Add the lemon juice and the pasta, and toss well. If necessary, thin the sauce with pasta cooking water. Serve in warmed shallow bowls.

Step 1

Step 4

Step 5

Preparation: 20 minutes
Cooking: 20 minutes
Per serving: 737 cal; 21 g pro;
31 g fat; 94 g carb.

TYPICALLY EMILIA-ROMAGNA
The people of Emilia-Romagna take their pasta seriously, but sometimes their playful side is realized in the array of rainbow-hued pastas available. For fun and variety, spinach, saffron, beet juice, and squid ink are used to color and flavor the noodles.

COOKING TIP

If you are using mature spinach with especially large leaves, simply chop before cooking (trim off the large stems). Large leaves tend to clump up and do not stir into the sauce well.

SERVING TIPS

With your meal, enjoy a crisp radicchio salad with thin rings of sweet onion and a classic vinaigrette.

🍷 Treat yourself to an excellent Tuscan white wine—a Galestro, for example.

SERVING TIPS Pass additional freshly grated or
shredded imported Parmesan cheese at the table.

Serve a Sicilian red wine, such as Corvo or Etna
Rosso, or offer a sparkling red grape juice.

FETTUCCINE WITH SICILIAN MEATBALLS

ITALY

Here's a down-home version of a classic Italian comfort food. Parmesan cheese and a dash of spice lend an enticing accent to these robust meatballs.

INGREDIENTS
(Serves 6)

- 1 hard roll
- ½ cup milk
- 2 slices prosciutto (1½ ounces) or other ham
- 1 pound ground beef or meatloaf mix
- 1 egg plus 1 egg yolk
- 2 tablespoons grated Parmesan
- salt and black pepper
- pinch of cayenne pepper
- 7 tablespoons olive oil
- 1 pound tricolor fettuccine
- 1 garlic clove
- fresh sage leaves
- juice of ½ lemon

INGREDIENT TIP
If you like, replace the sage with basil or oregano.

1 Break the roll into small pieces, place ¾ cup pieces in a medium bowl, and add the milk. Toss to evenly moisten the bread. Set aside to soak.

2 Cut the prosciutto into cubes and place in a large bowl. Add the meat, egg, egg yolk, Parmesan, 1½ teaspoons salt, ½ teaspoon pepper, and the cayenne. Squeeze the bread, add to the meat and mix well. Form into 1-inch balls.

3 Heat 3 tablespoons oil in a large skillet and brown the meatballs on all sides, about 10 minutes. Remove to a plate.

4 Meanwhile, cook the pasta in a large saucepan of boiling salted water according to the directions on the package until al dente.

5 Peel and mince the garlic and chop the sage. Add the remaining oil to the drippings in the skillet, and sauté the garlic and sage over medium heat-high heat for 2 minutes. Drain the pasta and add to the skillet. Add the meatballs and lemon juice, toss, and divide among serving plates.

Step 1

Step 2

Step 3

Preparation: 40 minutes
Cooking: 20 minutes
Per serving: 740 cal; 29 g pro; 41 g fat; 63 g carb.

TYPICALLY SICILIAN
On the balmy island of Sicily, citrus groves yield an abundance of bright, juicy lemons. These refreshing fruits add a burst of tangy flavor to many a Sicilian dish.

CLASSIC ITALIAN PESTO FETTUCCINE

ITALY

Nothing tastes of summer sun quite like fresh basil, the featured ingredient in this fragrant sauce. Here, Parmesan is mixed with slightly pungent pecorino for full-bodied flavor.

INGREDIENTS
(Serves 6)

- 2 garlic cloves
- salt
- ½ cup pine nuts or almonds
- 1 cup fresh basil leaves
- ½ cup grated Parmesan
- ¼ cup grated pecorino
- ¾ cup olive oil
- 1 pound fettuccine

INGREDIENT TIP

The flavor of pesto comes not only from the basil, pine nuts, and olive oil, but also from the cheese. Try mixing Parmesan, which is fairly mild, with the stronger-flavored pecorino. If you like, use ¾ cup of only one of these cheeses—Parmesan for a milder pesto or pecorino for a tangier, sharper sauce.

1 Peel the garlic and mash with the pine nuts and ½ teaspoon salt with a mortar and pestle (or use a blender). Remove the stems from the basil, and cut the leaves into strips. Add the basil to the garlic mixture and pound or blend to a puree. Gradually blend in both of the cheeses.

2 Add the olive oil, at first drop by drop, and then in a thin stream, while stirring or blending on low speed, until the mixture is a thick paste.

3 Meanwhile, cook the fettuccine in a large saucepan of boiling salted water according to the directions on the package until al dente.

4 Drain the pasta in a colander and place in a large warmed bowl. Add the pesto and toss to coat thoroughly. Divide among 6 plates and serve immediately.

Step 1

Step 2

Step 4

Preparation: 35 minutes
Cooking: 20 minutes
Per serving: 630 cal; 17 g pro; 37 g fat; 59 g carb.

TYPICALLY LIGURIAN

There are many versions of the famous pesto sauce that hails from the coastal Italian region of Liguria. The recipes vary from each other only slightly. For example, you might find a pesto with walnuts and parsley, or one with bits of tomato.

COOKING TIPS

- Toast the pine nuts for a nuttier flavored sauce.
- Cover fresh pesto with olive oil and store in the refrigerator for up to 2 weeks.
- When fresh basil is abundant, create a reserve for winter: Freeze the sauce in plastic food storage bags or the sections of an ice-cube tray.

SERVING TIPS

Tiramisu, the classic Italian mascarpone cream cake, makes an excellent conclusion to the meal.

Serve a light white wine, such as Verdicchio, or iced tea with a sprig of fresh mint.

$\mathscr{S}$AVORY GREEK-STYLE RIGATONI

GREECE

INGREDIENTS
(Serves 6)

- 1 pound small cucumbers
- 1 onion
- 4 bacon strips
- 2 tablespoons olive oil
- ⅔ cup heavy cream
- salt and white pepper
- 1 pound rigatoni
- 8 ounces feta cheese
- fresh basil leaves (optional)

INGREDIENT TIP

If you like, you can try this dish with zucchini instead of cucumbers.

Fresh, crumbly feta cheese and crisp cucumbers are favored ingredients in Greek cuisine. Both are irresistibly combined in a rich, cheesy sauce flavored with bacon.

1 Peel the cucumbers so that thin strips of peel remain at regular intervals. Cut the cucumbers in half lengthwise, scoop out the seeds with a small spoon, and cut crosswise into ¼-inch-thick pieces. Peel and finely chop the onion. Cut the bacon crosswise into small pieces.

Step 1

2 Heat the oil in a large saucepan and sauté the bacon over medium heat for 2 minutes. Add the onion; sauté until translucent, about 5 minutes. Place the cream in a small saucepan; heat to boiling over medium-high heat. Then simmer over low heat until reduced by half, about 5 minutes.

3 Add the cucumber, ½ teaspoon salt, and ¼ teaspoon white pepper to the bacon mixture. Sauté until cooked but not soft, about 4 minutes.

Step 1

4 Meanwhile, cook the rigatoni in a large saucepan of boiling salted water according to the directions on the package until al dente. Crumble the cheese.

5 Drain the pasta. Stir the cheese and cream into the cucumber mixture. Add the pasta and garnish with basil.

Step 5

Preparation: 25 minutes
Cooking: 20 minutes
Per serving: 616 cal; 17 g pro; 33 g fat; 63 g carb.

TYPICALLY GREEK

The Greeks are fond of cheese—they consume a host of local, regional varieties. One of their favorites is feta, the tangy, pure white cheese originally made from sheep's milk but now produced from cow or goat's milk as well.

COOKING TIPS

• If you want a more strongly seasoned dish, add a clove or two of fresh garlic. Just use a garlic press to mash it, then sauté it with the onion in Step 2.

• Reserve ½ cup pasta cooking water to mix with the pasta and sauce if the mixture is too thick after tossing together.

SERVING TIPS

Kataifi, a pastry made with a shredded dough and a sweet nut filling, is a popular dessert in Greece.

🍷 Accompany this dish with a light white wine or sparkling grape juice.

*T*OMATO SAUCE—THREE WAYS

Try our trio of tomato-sauces—hearty, light, and creamy—with a pound of spaghetti. We've imported each recipe from a different region of Italy.

ZESTY MARINARA SAUCE

Preparation: 25 minutes   Cooking: 15 minutes

CALABRIA

(SERVES 4)
- 2¼ pounds fresh plum tomatoes
- 1 red onion
- 2–3 garlic cloves
- 2 tablespoons olive oil
- ¼ –½ teaspoon crushed red pepper
- ¼ cup red wine
- salt and black pepper

1 In a large saucepan of boiling water, blanch the tomatoes. Place in a bowl of cold water. Peel, seed, and cube the tomatoes, and place in a medium bowl.

2 Peel the onion and garlic; thinly slice. Heat the oil in a large skillet over medium-high heat and sauté the onion, garlic, and crushed pepper until the onion is translucent, about 5 minutes.

3 Add the cubed tomatoes, wine, ½ teaspoon salt, and ¼ teaspoon black pepper, and simmer for 8–10 minutes, until thickened.

QUICK BASIL AND

Preparation: 10 minutes

LIGURIA

(SERVES 4)
- 2¼ pounds fresh plum tomatoes
- 2 tablespoons butter
- salt and pepper
- a few fresh basil leaves

1 In a large saucepan of boiling water, blanch the tomatoes. Place in a bowl of cold water. Peel, seed, and cube the tomatoes, and place in a medium bowl.

CREAMY BACON-TOMATO SAUCE

Preparation: 15 minutes   Cooking: 25 minutes

LAZIO

(SERVES 4)
- 2 pounds fresh plum tomatoes
- 2 bacon strips
- 1 small onion
- 1 tablespoon olive oil
- salt and pepper
- 4-5 tablespoons heavy cream

1 In a large saucepan of boiling water, blanch the tomatoes. Place in a bowl of cold water. Peel, seed, and cube the tomatoes, and place in a medium bowl.

2 Cut the bacon crosswise into thin pieces. Peel and finely chop the onion.

3 Heat the oil in a large skillet over medium heat, and sauté the bacon for 4 minutes, until crisp. Add the onion and sauté for 6 minutes, until translucent. Add the tomatoes, ½ teaspoon salt, and ¼ teaspoon pepper.

4 Cover; simmer over low heat for 10 minutes, until thickened. Stir in the cream.

5 Pour the sauce through a sieve and reheat before tossing with the pasta.

TOMATO SAUCE

Cooking: 5 minutes

2 Melt the butter in a large skillet over medium heat. Add the tomatoes, 1 teaspoon salt, and ¼ teaspoon pepper and sauté for 3–4 minutes, until the tomatoes are soft.

3 Tear the basil into small pieces or finely slice. Just before serving, stir the basil into the sauce.

CARAMELIZED-ONION SPAETZLE

GERMANY

Here's a rustic specialty from Germany's Alps. Small homemade spaetzle noodles are cooked casserole-style with mild Swiss cheese and crispy fried onions.

INGREDIENTS
(Serves 4)

FOR THE SPAETZLE
- 4 large eggs
- ½ cup milk
- 1½ teaspoons salt
- ½ teaspoon nutmeg
- 3 cups all-purpose flour

IN ADDITION
- ½ pound Emmentaler or other Swiss cheese
- 1 medium onion
- 3 tablespoons butter

INGREDIENT TIPS
- You can try Gouda or Gruyère in place of Emmentaler or Swiss cheese.
- For a slightly different flavor and crispier texture, try substituting 3 medium shallots for the onion.

1 Preheat the oven to 300ºF. Mix the eggs, milk, salt, and nutmeg together in a large bowl. Add the flour and mix until very smooth. Let the dough stand for 10 minutes.

2 Meanwhile, bring a large pot of salted water to a boil over high heat. Grate the cheese and set it aside.

3 Press the dough through a spaetzle maker directly into the boiling water. Reduce the heat and allow the spaetzle to cook until they rise to the surface, about 5 minutes. With a slotted spoon, remove the spaetzle from the water and allow to drain.

4 Place half the spaetzle in a casserole dish and top with half the cheese. Repeat layering once. Cover the casserole dish with aluminum foil and place in the oven to keep warm while preparing the onions.

5 Peel the onion and cut into thin slices. Melt the butter in a skillet and fry the onion slices over medium heat until they are golden brown, about 15 minutes. Cover the spaetzle with the caramelized onion and serve immediately.

Step 3

Step 3

Step 4

Preparation: 30 minutes
Cooking: 25 minutes
Per serving: 729 cal; 33 g pro; 31 g fat; 77 g carb.

TYPICALLY GERMAN
This rich, homey dish originated in Germany's idyllic southern Alps, a region of rolling heights and grazing terrain for many of the country's dairy cows. The milk, butter, and cheese produced here are of very fine quality.

COOKING TIPS

- If you don't have a spaetzle maker, try using a potato ricer to press the dough into the boiling water. A colander and rubber spatula also work, but they require an extra set of hands.
- If the spaetzle clump together while cooking, stir vigorously until they separate.

SERVING TIPS

These noodles are wonderful served with a fresh lettuce and cucumber salad dressed with oil and vinegar.

Try this with a fruit juice spritzer—apple is especially nice.

SERVING TIPS A loaf of crusty bread and some fresh butter is all you need with this tasty dish.

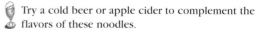 Try a cold beer or apple cider to complement the flavors of these noodles.

SPINACH & MEAT-STUFFED NOODLES

GERMANY

Here, pasta dumplings are filled with spinach and meat and cooked and served in beef broth. Topped with sautéed onions and fresh chives, this hearty dish is a favorite in Germany.

INGREDIENTS
(Serves 4)

- 3 cups all-purpose flour
- salt and pepper
- 5 large eggs
- 1 tablespoon olive oil
- 2 day-old rolls, cubed
- ½ cup milk
- 3 bacon strips, chopped
- 1½ cups chopped onion
- ½ pound fresh spinach
- ¼ pound sweet Italian sausage, casing removed, crumbled
- 1 tablespoon butter
- 8 cups beef broth
- 1 tablespoon chopped fresh chives

INGREDIENT TIP

You can substitute half of a 10-ounce box of thawed frozen chopped spinach for the fresh spinach.

1 On a work surface, mix the flour and 1 teaspoon salt. Make a well in the center and add 4 eggs, 3 tablespoons ice water, and the oil. Mix with a fork and your fingers, then knead until smooth and elastic, 10 minutes. Cover; let rest for 10 minutes.

2 In a bowl, mix the bread and milk. In a skillet over medium heat, cook the bacon and ½ cup onion for 5 minutes. Cook the spinach for 3 minutes in a large saucepan of boiling water; drain, chop, and place in a large bowl. Squeeze the milk from the bread. Add the bread to the spinach. Add the bacon mixture, sausage, remaining egg, and ½ teaspoon *each* salt and pepper; mix.

3 On a floured surface, in batches, roll out the dough ¹⁄₁₆-inch thick. Cut into 2 x 4-inch rectangles. Top each with 1 tablespoon spinach mixture, dampen the edges and seal.

4 In a skillet, sauté the remaining onion in the butter over medium-high heat until golden, 7 minutes. In a large saucepan, boil the broth, add the pasta and cook until tender, 12 minutes. Serve the pasta and broth with the sautéed onions and chives.

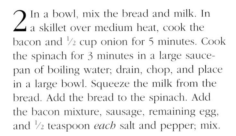

Step 2

Step 3

Step 4

Preparation: 55 minutes
Cooking: 20 minutes
Per serving: 842 cal; 31 g pro; 35 g fat; 98 g carb.

TYPICALLY GERMAN

Germans are well-known beer afficianados, but many are wine lovers too. Carefully tended vineyards produce the wines that often accompany regional dishes like this dumpling soup.

ROAST DUCK OVER ORANGE NOODLES

FRANCE

In this dish—inspired by the famous duck à l'orange—tender slices of roasted meat top fine vermicelli noodles. Green peppercorns and orange juice accent the lightly creamy sauce.

INGREDIENTS
(Serves 4)

- 3 oranges
- 1 teaspoon drained green peppercorns (in brine)
- 4 duck breasts (about 5 ounces each)
- salt and black pepper
- 1 pound vermicelli
- 3 tablespoons olive oil

IN ADDITION

- 4 fresh tarragon sprigs, for garnish

INGREDIENT TIP

Slightly crunchy, preserved green peppercorns are sold packed in brine in small jars. If you can't get any, feel free to substitute an additional ½ teaspoon freshly ground black pepper in the dressing.

1 Squeeze the oranges to get 1 cup of juice; place in a small saucepan with the green peppercorns. Bring to a simmer; continue cooking until reduced to ⅔ cup, about 7 minutes. Let cool.

2 Preheat the oven to 400°F. Place the duck breasts skin-side up on a cutting board. Cut diagonal slashes across the skin. Sprinkle the duck breasts with ½ teaspoon salt and ¼ teaspoon black pepper.

Step 2

3 Heat a large ovenproof skillet over medium heat. Add the duck skin-side down; cook for 4 minutes. Place in the oven and roast for 2 minutes; turn and cook for 2 minutes more. Transfer to a clean board.

Step 4

4 Cook the vermicelli in a large pot of boiling salted water until al dente. Meanwhile in a large bowl, whisk together the olive oil and reduced orange juice. Add ½ teaspoon salt and ¼ teaspoon black pepper. Drain the pasta, add to the bowl and toss. Divide among 4 dinner plates.

Step 5

5 Thinly slice the duck breasts on the diagonal, then arrange on top of the pasta. Garnish with tarragon and serve.

Preparation: 15 minutes
Cooking: 20 minutes
Per serving: 539 cal; 15 g pro;
12 g fat; 91 g carb.

TYPICALLY FRENCH

The French adore tender poultry, and duck, with its strong, unique flavor, has a particular appeal for them. Ducks—Rouen, Nantes, and Barbary breeds are particularly favored—are magically transformed into the most delightful delicacies.

COOKING TIPS

• Brown the duck breast first on its skin side and turn it only once, when the skin is crispy.

• In order to make your time in the kitchen less hectic, you can cook the duck an hour ahead. Place on a plate and cover loosely with foil. This way, you'll have plenty of time to cook the noodles.

SERVING TIPS

If you like, try adding a shot of orange liqueur to the skillet when cooking the duck. And you can garnish the plate with orange segments.

🍷 A hearty red wine such as a Bordeaux or Burgundy rounds out this dish.

ℋUNGARIAN PAPRIKA NOODLES

HUNGARY

INGREDIENTS
(Serves 4)

- 2 *each* red, yellow, and green bell peppers
- 1 small onion
- 2 garlic cloves
- 1 pound elbow macaroni
- 3 tablespoons olive oil
- 1 teaspoon paprika
- 1 teaspoon dried thyme
- ½ bay leaf
- salt and black pepper
- 1 cup chicken broth
- 2 tablespoons butter
- 1 tablespoon chopped parsley

INGREDIENT TIP
You can use just about any short pasta for this dish: farfalle, shells, or smooth or ridged ziti, penne, or rigatoni.

This light, delicious sauce from Hungary tastes as vibrant as it looks. It's the contrasting flavors of the sweet bell peppers and bold, spicy paprika that lend this dish particular allure.

1 Preheat the oven to 400°F. For the sauce, cut the bell peppers lengthwise into fourths, seed, and rinse in cold water. Place skin-side up on a baking sheet. Roast for 15 minutes, until the skins begin to blister.

2 Peel the onion and garlic and thinly slice. Remove the peppers from the oven, place in a bowl, and cover. Let stand for a few minutes. Peel the peppers and cut into small cubes.

3 Cook the noodles in a large saucepan of boiling salted water according to the directions on the package until al dente.

4 Meanwhile, heat the oil in a large saucepan over medium-high heat and sauté the onion and garlic until the onions are translucent, about 5 minutes. Stir in the cubed peppers, paprika, thyme, bay leaf, ½ teaspoon salt, and ¼ teaspoon black pepper. Add the broth, heat to boiling, cover, and simmer over medium-low heat for 10 minutes.

5 Drain the noodles in a colander and return to the pan. Add the onion-pepper sauce, butter, and parsley and toss to coat.

Step 1

Step 2

Step 4

Preparation: 45 minutes
Cooking: 20 minutes
Per serving: 616 cal; 17 g pro; 19 g fat; 96 g carb.

TYPICALLY HUNGARIAN
Paprika, ground dried sweet red peppers, is a distinctive seasoning of Hungarian cuisine and a significant export. The largest areas of paprika production are around Szeged, a city in the south of Hungary.

COOKING TIPS

• Red, green, and yellow bell peppers vary as to how long they must remain in the oven before their skin blisters—so keep checking on them!

• You can remove the skins more easily if you cover the peppers in a bowl or place them in a paper or plastic bag and let rest for 10 minutes.

SERVING TIPS

A bowl with peppers of different colors and varieties makes an eye-catching centerpiece.

🍷 Offer a dry Hungarian Tokaji (Tokay) or another light white wine with a full bouquet.

SPICY PENNE AND BROCCOLI

USA

This terrific one-dish meal is popular across America. Garlic and spicy chile peppers are lively seasonings for the tender broccoli florets, toasted pine nuts, and penne pasta.

INGREDIENTS
(Serves 4)

- 1 bunch broccoli
- 2 garlic cloves
- 2 small red hot chiles or ½ teaspoon crushed red pepper
- 6 anchovies (optional)
- 1 pound penne
- ¼ cup pine nuts or almonds
- ½ cup olive oil, preferably extra virgin
- salt and black pepper

INGREDIENT TIP

Cauliflower and zucchini are also suitable for this dish. Let the season guide your choice. This dish tastes great with the addition of cooked shrimp, Italian sausage, diced turkey, or chunks of chicken.

1 Cut the broccoli into florets. Peel the stalks and slice into ¼-inch thick coins. Cook both in simmering water (or steam) until crisp-tender, about 5 minutes. Drain, then cool under running water.

2 Peel and mince the garlic. Mince the red chile. Rinse the anchovies with cold water, then cut them into small pieces.

3 Cook the penne in a large pot of boiling salted water, stirring often, until al dente. Set aside ½ cup of the pasta cooking water, then drain the pasta. Meanwhile, in a large dry skillet over medium heat, roast the pine nuts, stirring occasionally, until toasted. Transfer to a plate.

4 Add the olive oil to the skillet. Add the garlic and minced chile and stir over medium-low heat for 3 minutes, until the garlic is barely colored. Stir in the anchovies and broccoli; heat through over medium-high heat, stirring.

5 Add the penne and reserved pasta cooking water to the broccoli mixture. Season with salt and black pepper and toss well. Sprinkle with the pine nuts and serve.

Step 1

Step 3

Step 5

Preparation: 25 minutes
Cooking: 20 minutes
Per serving: 739 cal; 20 g pro; 35 g fat; 92 g carb.

TYPICALLY AMERICAN
Brought to the New World by Italian immigrants, broccoli has become an American favorite. This cool-weather crop is grown across the country in home gardens and the giant fields of California.

Cooking Tip

If you like, add diced fresh tomatoes—the sweet, tangy juices will stretch the sauce a little farther. You can sauté them with the broccoli in Step 4.

Serving Tips

Offer grated cheese on the side, preferably a full-flavored, aged Parmesan or pecorino.

 Try this dish with a light Californian white wine, such as a Sauvignon Blanc.

SERVING TIPS Offer a fresh mixed salad of tomato, cucumber, and spring herbs.

For refreshment, serve a chilled Californian Chardonnay or mineral water.

*B*OW TIES PRIMAVERA

USA

Celebrate the season's first harvest with a sauce of tender green asparagus, fresh mushrooms, sugar snap peas, and carrots. Bow-tie shaped pasta adds to the appeal of this dish.

INGREDIENTS
(Serves 4)

- ½ pound asparagus
- ¼ pound white button mushrooms
- 6 ounces sugar snap peas
- ¼ pound prosciutto
- 1 slender carrot
- 1 pound bow ties or penne
- 2 tablespoons *each* butter and olive oil
- 1 cup frozen early peas
- 1 cup heavy cream
- ½ cup dry white wine
- salt and black pepper
- pinch *each* of nutmeg and dried marjoram or oregano

INGREDIENT TIP
When asparagus and peas are used in a dish, it is often called "primavera," but other early vegetables—scallions, Chinese pea pods, spinach, Swiss chard—can be used.

1 Rinse the asparagus, trim off the tough ends and peel the lower third. Cut the stalks diagonally into 1½-inch pieces. In a large saucepan of boiling water, cook the asparagus for 3 minutes, remove to a bowl of ice water, and let stand until cool.

2 Wipe the mushrooms with a damp paper towel and cut into quarters. Rinse the snap peas, pat dry and cut into strips. Cut the prosciutto into strips. Dice the carrot.

3 Cook the bow ties in a large saucepan of boiling salted water according to the directions on the package until al dente.

4 Meanwhile, melt the butter in the oil in a large skillet over medium heat. Sauté the mushrooms, snap peas, carrot, and early peas for 4 minutes. Add the prosciutto and cook for 3 minutes. Stir in the cream and wine. Heat to boiling and simmer for 5 minutes.

5 Stir ½ teaspoon salt, ¼ teaspoon black pepper, the nutmeg, and marjoram into the sauce. Drain the asparagus and pasta and add to the sauce. Toss to coat and mix.

Step 1

Step 2

Step 4

Preparation: 30 minutes
Cooking: 20 minutes
Per serving: 896 cal; 29 g pro; 41 g fat; 100 g carb.

TYPICALLY LITTLE ITALY
In the many Italian restaurants of Manhattan's Little Italy—famous for its lively atmosphere and colorful street crowd—you can find pasta in all its classic and modern variations.

𝒮PAGHETTI TETRAZZINI

USA

A scrumptious creamy chicken ragu crowns this crisp noodle casserole, an American favorite. It's a heartwarming treat that's sure to please family and friends.

INGREDIENTS
(Serves 4)

- 1 onion
- 5 tablespoons butter
- ½ cup white wine
- 2 cups chicken broth
- 1 pound skinless boneless chicken breasts
- ½ bay leaf
- 1 pound spaghetti
- 1 tablespoon flour
- ⅔ cup heavy cream
- 2 tablespoons lemon juice
- 1 egg yolk
- salt and white pepper
- ¼ cup grated Parmesan

INGREDIENT TIPS

- Skinless boneless turkey can replace the chicken.
- You can omit the wine and use 2½ cups chicken broth as the poaching liquid.

1 Peel and finely chop the onion. In a large saucepan, melt 1 tablespoon butter over medium-high heat. Add the onion and sauté until translucent, about 5 minutes. Add the wine and boil for 1 minute. Add the broth, chicken, and bay leaf. Cover and simmer over low heat until the chicken is cooked through, about 10 minutes. Cut into ¾-inch cubes. Reserve the cooking liquid.

2 Cook the pasta in a large pot of boiling salted water until al dente. Melt 2 tablespoons butter in a medium saucepan over medium heat. Add the flour and cook for 1 minute, stirring. Stir in the cooking liquid (discard the bay leaf) and simmer for 1 minute. In a small bowl, mix the cream, lemon juice, egg yolk, and ¼ teaspoon *each* salt and pepper. Stir into the sauce. Cool for 5 minutes.

3 Preheat the oven to 450°F. In a greased 10-inch round baking dish, mix the pasta with half the sauce. Make a well in the center. Add the chicken to the remaining sauce and pour into the pasta well. Dot the pasta with the remaining butter and sprinkle with the cheese. Bake for 20 minutes.

Step 1

Step 2

Step 3

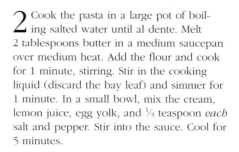

Preparation: 25 minutes
Cooking: 20 minutes
Per serving: 899 cal; 46 g pro; 37 g fat; 93 g carb.

TYPICALLY CALIFORNIAN
This exquisite pasta and chicken dish was created to honor an Italian opera diva, Luisa Tetrazzini, around the turn of the century. Although its place of origin is not truly known, some say it is San Francisco.

COOKING TIP

Cooking flour in butter forms a a light roux, the base of many sauces. To mix it properly, add the flour gradually to the butter, stirring constantly, until it foams. Keep stirring until the roux has turned a golden yellow color. Then pour in the broth.

SERVING TIPS

Offer refreshing fruit sorbet in attractive dessert goblets for a luscious ending to this meal. Serve crunchy wafer cookies alongside.

 Enjoy a glass of Oregon Pinot Noir or iced tea with the main course.

PROSCIUTTO PARMESAN PAPPARDELLE

AUSTRALIA

Pappardelle, a wide ribbon noodle, is combined here with a luscious prosciutto cream sauce and finished with Parmesan cheese. It's the perfect dish for a no-fuss lunch or dinner.

INGREDIENTS
(Serves 4)

- ½ pound sliced prosciutto or country ham
- 1 pound pappardelle
- 3 tablespoons butter
- ¾ cup heavy cream
- ¾ cup reduced-sodium chicken broth or pasta cooking water
- ground white pepper
- 3 ounces freshly grated Parmesan cheese

IN ADDITION
- ½ bunch chives

INGREDIENT TIP

If desired, you can omit the meat and add a mixture of blanched seasonal vegetables to the cream sauce. Be sure to season with enough salt.

1 With a large sharp knife, slice the prosciutto into ½-inch-wide strips, then cut into dice.

2 Cook the pappardelle in a large pot of boiling salted water until al dente. Meanwhile, in a medium saucepan, melt the butter over medium-low heat. Add the ham and cook for 2 minutes.

3 Pour in the cream and broth. Bring to a simmer, taking care not to let the mixture boil over. Cook for 5 minutes longer to reduce slightly.

4 Drain the noodles well and toss gently with the warm cream sauce. Season to taste with white pepper. Sprinkle the Parmesan on top and toss again.

5 Divide the pappardelle among 4 warmed plates. Finely chop the chives. Sprinkle over the pasta and serve immediately.

Step 1

Step 4

Step 5

Preparation: 10 minutes
Cooking: 20 minutes
Per serving: 869 cal; 40 g pro;
40 g fat; 87 g carb.

TYPICALLY AUSTRALIAN
In the original recipe for this dish, called *pappardelle con la lepre* in Italy, the sauce was prepared with rabbit. Italian settlers in Australia created a version that used ham as a substitute.

COOKING TIP

Since prosciutto can be quite salty, you don't need to add any salt to the sauce. For a delicious treat, try a pappardelle casserole. Add 1 egg yolk to the finished sauce, sprinkle with bread crumbs, and bake in a 375°F oven for 20 minutes, until brown and bubbly.

SERVING TIPS

As an appetizer, offer a colorful chilled seafood salad, complemented by a lemon vinaigrette.

 Australian white wine from the Barossa Valley pairs well with these flavors.

CREAMY SAUCE—THREE WAYS

Everybody loves pasta in a mouthwatering sauce. Here we
offer you three sensational variations—seafood from Spain,
peppers from the USA, and a version of carbonara from Italy.

GARLIC SHRIMP LINGUINE

Preparation: 5 minutes   Cooking: 20 minutes

SPAIN

(SERVES 4)
- 1 pound linguine
- 6 scallions
- 1 garlic clove
- 1$\frac{2}{3}$ pounds shrimp
- 2 tablespoons olive oil
- $\frac{2}{3}$ cup heavy cream
- 1$\frac{1}{2}$ teaspoons lemon juice
- salt and white pepper

1 In a large saucepan of boiling salted water, cook the linguine according to the directions on the package until al dente.

2 Meanwhile, trim the root and tough green portion from the scallions and cut the remainder into thin rings. Peel and mince the garlic, then shell and devein the shrimp.

3 In a large skillet, heat the oil over medium-high heat and sauté the scallions and garlic for 2 minutes. Add the shrimp and sauté just until they turn pink, 2–3 minutes. Stir in the cream, lemon juice, 1 teaspoon salt, and $\frac{1}{4}$ teaspoon pepper.

4 Drain the linguine in a colander. Add to the shrimp mixture. Toss well.

BELL PEPPER

Preparation: 5 minutes

USA

(SERVES 4)
- 1 pound bow-tie pasta
- 1 *each* red and green bell pepper
- 1 onion
- 2 tablespoons olive oil
- $\frac{1}{3}$ cup heavy cream
- salt and white pepper
- pinch of cayenne

1 In a large saucepan of boiling salted water, cook the bow ties according to the directions on the package until al dente.

BOW TIES

Cooking: 20 minutes

---

2 Meanwhile, cut the bell peppers in half, seed, and cut into ½-inch cubes. Peel and dice the onion.

3 In a large skillet, heat the oil over medium-high heat and sauté the peppers and onion until they soften, about 10 minutes. Stir in the cream, 1 teaspoon salt, ¼ teaspoon white pepper, and the cayenne.

4 Drain the bow ties in a colander, and add to the pepper mixture. Toss gently until well mixed.

SPINACH SPAGHETTI WITH BACON

Preparation: 5 minutes   Cooking: 20 minutes

ITALY

(SERVES 4)
- 1 pound spinach spaghetti
- 10 bacon strips
- ⅓ cup heavy cream
- ⅓ cup grated Parmesan
- white pepper

1 In a large saucepan of boiling salted water, cook the spaghetti according to the directions on the package until al dente.

2 Cut the bacon crosswise into small pieces. In a large skillet, sauté the bacon over medium heat until crisp, about 5 minutes. Leave 2 tablespoons bacon drippings and the bacon in the pan.

3 Drain the spaghetti in a colander; add to the bacon. Toss to coat. Add the cream, Parmesan, and ¼ teaspoon white pepper, and toss.

SERVING TIPS For seasoning to individual taste, soy sauce is a must at the table.

 Green tea goes very well with this dish, as do rice wine or medium-bodied white wine.

SINGAPORE NOODLES AND SHRIMP

SINGAPORE

Ginger, garlic, and hot chiles are popular seasonings of delicious Singaporean cuisine. Here, these spices lend vibrant flavor to crisp vegetables, tender shrimp, and egg noodles.

INGREDIENTS
(Serves 4)

- ½ pound Chinese egg noodles
- ½ pound shrimp
- 2 carrots
- 2 scallions
- 1 yellow bell pepper
- 2 jalapeño chiles
- 2-inch piece fresh ginger
- 1 garlic clove
- 3 tablespoons oil
- 1 cup mung bean sprouts
- 4-5 tablespoons soy sauce

INGREDIENT TIPS

- Refresh the bean sprouts before use in a bowl of ice-cold water so that they regain their crispness.
- Vary the vegetables with water chestnuts, bamboo sprouts, and Chinese baby corn. Add soy sauce, salt, and pepper according to the selection.

1 In a large saucepan of boiling salted water, cook the noodles for 2 minutes, or according to the package directions. Drain well in a colander.

2 Peel and devein the shrimp. Peel the carrots and cut into long thin strips. Trim the root and tough green portion of the scallions and cut the remainder crosswise into rings. Seed the bell pepper and dice.

3 Seed and finely chop the jalapeños. Peel the ginger and cut into fine strips. Peel and mince the garlic.

4 Heat the oil in a wok or large skillet over high heat and stir-fry the jalapeños, ginger, and garlic for 1 minute. Add the shrimp and stir-fry for 3 minutes. Remove the mixture to a bowl.

5 Add the vegetables, ¾ cup water, and 4 tablespoons soy sauce to the wok and stir-fry for 3 minutes. Add the noodles and bean sprouts and mix well. Add the shrimp mixture and stir-fry for 1 minute. Stir in the remaining soy sauce, if desired.

Step 1

Step 3

Step 5

Preparation: 35 minutes
Cooking: 10 minutes
Per serving: 376 cal; 18 g pro; 12 g fat; 53 g carb.

TYPICALLY SINGAPORE

Singapore, with its bustling harbor, is one of the greatest trading centers of the world. The famous "night market" is a gourmet's paradise in which one can find exotic delicacies from all over the globe.

NOODLES WITH SHIITAKE MUSHROOMS

JAPAN

This light vegetarian dish from the land of the cherry blossoms is distinguished by its delicacy and charming presentation. The homemade noodles are simple to prepare.

INGREDIENTS
(Serves 4)

FOR THE NOODLES
- 2 cups unbleached all-purpose flour
- ½ teaspoon salt
- 3 large eggs

FOR THE TOPPING
- 1 pound fresh shiitake mushrooms
- 2 tablespoons peanut oil
- 1 pint cherry tomatoes
- salt and pepper
- ¼ cup chopped fresh basil
- 2 tablespoons fresh lime juice
- 2 tablespoons Asian sesame oil

INGREDIENT TIP

If shiitakes are unavailable, use another flavorful fresh mushroom: oyster, cremini and portobello are suitable.

1 On a work surface, toss together 1¼ cups of the flour and the salt. Form into a mound and make a well in the center. Add the eggs and gradually work them into the flour with your fingers until incorporated. Knead the dough, adding more flour as necessary, until smooth and elastic, about 8 minutes. Cover and let rest for 10 minutes.

Step 1

2 Bring a large pot of salted water to a boil. Meanwhile, trim off each mushroom stem and thinly slice the caps. Heat the oil in a large skillet over medium heat. Add the mushrooms; cook, stirring, until browned, about 5 minutes. Stir in the tomatoes. Let rest off the heat.

Step 3

3 Roll out the dough to a ⅛-inch thickness. Cut into ¼-inch-wide noodles. Add to the boiling water and cook, stirring often, for 3 minutes. Drain well.

4 Warm the mushrooms and tomatoes over high heat. Stir in ½ teaspoon salt and ¼ teaspoon pepper. Add the pasta and toss well. Add the basil, lime juice, and sesame oil. Toss well and serve.

Step 4

Preparation: 20 minutes
Cooking: 10 minutes
Per serving: 443 cal; 14 g pro; 18 g fat; 57 g carb.

TYPICALLY JAPANESE
Noodles are nearly as popular as rice in Japan, and may be eaten hot or cold. They reflect regional variations as well: Fat wheat noodles are popular in the south while buckwheat noodles are standard Tokyo fare.

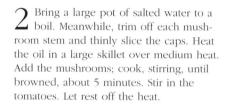

COOKING TIP

If you'd like to make your work easier, crank the
noodle dough through a pasta machine. Or purchase
ready-made dried rice noodles, available at any Asian
food market. Adjust the cooking time, since dried
noodles take a longer time to cook than fresh ones.

SERVING TIPS

Tableware in Japan often includes
decorative lacquered bowls and
matching chopsticks.

 Serve a light aromatic green tea or sake
with this meal.

CRISPY NOODLE-AND-PORK STIR-FRY

INGREDIENTS
(Serves 4)

FOR THE MARINADE
- 1½-inch piece fresh ginger
- pinch of sugar
- 1 teaspoon *each* soy sauce, oyster sauce, and Asian sesame oil

FOR THE STIR-FRY
- ½ pound boneless pork loin
- 1 bunch of scallions
- 1 garlic clove
- ½ pound Chinese egg noodles
- 5 tablespoons oil
- 1 cup chicken broth
- 1 tablespoon cornstarch
- 1 teaspoon *each* sugar, soy sauce, oyster sauce and Asian sesame oil

INGREDIENT TIP

Sliver an extra scallion and use as a garnish for the dish.

Pan-fried egg noodles create a tangled, crunchy nest for the savory marinated pork and fresh scallions in this quick-cooking, authentic Asian treat.

1 Peel and mince the ginger and mix with the remaining marinade ingredients in a large bowl. Cut the pork into finger-thick slices and marinate for at least 30 minutes or as long as 3 hours.

Step 1

2 Trim the scallions and cut into 2-inch lengths. Peel and mince the garlic. Cook the noodles in boiling salted water according to the directions on the package. Drain, rinse with cold water and pat dry.

Step 2

3 Heat half of the oil in a wok over medium-high heat. Add the noodles and fry until crispy, turning the noodles gently and patting them down occasionally so they brown evenly, about 8 minutes in all. Remove to a platter.

4 For the sauce, mix the chicken broth, cornstarch, sugar, soy sauce, oyster sauce, and sesame oil. Heat the remaining oil in the wok and stir-fry the garlic for 30 seconds. Add the pork and stir-fry for 2–3 minutes. Add the scallions and the sauce and stir-fry for 2 minutes, until the sauce thickens. Serve the meat in the center of the noodles.

Step 3

Marinating: 30 minutes
Preparation: 15 minutes
Cooking: 15 minutes
Per serving: 508 cal; 19 g pro; 28 g fat; 50 g carb.

TYPICALLY CHINESE
The wok is one of the most important tools in the Chinese kitchen. Since woks were originally used for cooking over an open fire, they are traditionally made with a rounded bottom, which optimizes heat distribution.

COOKING TIP

If you don't have a wok, you should use a cast-iron skillet for frying the noodles, since these heavy pans retain heat very well and can crisp the noodles as required in this recipe.

SERVING TIPS

This dish might be complemented by a salad of bamboo shoots, bean sprouts, and bok choy.

 Green tea is the recommended accompaniment, but you can also try a crisp white or red wine.

CASHEW SHRIMP VERMICELLI

CHINA

INGREDIENTS
(Serves 4)

- 1 ounce dried cloud ear, tree ear, or any other Chinese black mushroom
- 1 garlic clove
- 1-inch piece fresh ginger
- 2 scallions
- 2 carrots
- ½ cup snow peas
- 1 celery rib
- ½ pound unshelled shrimp
- ½ pound Asian vermicelli
- 6 tablespoons + ¼ cup oil
- ¼ cup cashew nuts
- pinch of Chinese five-spice powder (optional)
- ½ cup chicken broth
- 3 tablespoons oyster sauce

INGREDIENT TIP

Chinese five-spice powder is a blend of Szechuan peppercorns, cinnamon, cloves, fennel, and star anise. Add it to marinades, poaching syrup for fruit, and nut-bread batter.

This much-loved classic dish of Chinese cuisine tantalizes the taste buds with fried vermicelli noodles in a delicious medley of fresh vegetables and shrimp.

1 In a small bowl, soak the mushrooms in 1 cup warm water for 30 minutes. Peel and dice the garlic and ginger. Cut the scallions into small pieces. Cut the carrots into small dice. Cut the snow peas and celery into crosswise pieces.

2 Peel the shrimp, leaving the tails intact. Devein, rinse, and dry. Cook the noodles in a large saucepan of boiling salted water according to the directions on the package. Drain and spread out on wax paper. Drain the mushrooms and cut into quarters.

3 Heat 3 tablespoons oil in a wok or large skillet over high heat. Stir-fry the garlic and ginger for 30 seconds. Add the shrimp and stir-fry for 2 minutes. Remove to a plate.

4 Heat 3 tablespoons oil and stir-fry the vegetables, mushrooms, cashews, and five-spice powder for 1 minute. Add the broth, oyster sauce, and shrimp. Simmer for 2 minutes. Remove to a bowl; keep warm.

5 Heat the remaining ¼ cup oil and stir-fry the noodles until golden brown. Drain on paper towels, and place in a large shallow bowl. Top with the cashew shrimp.

Step 1

Step 2

Step 5

Preparation: 30 minutes
Cooking: 10 minutes
Per serving: 606 cal; 21 g pro; 33 g fat; 58 g carb.

TYPICALLY CHINESE
The seasoning of dishes in Chinese cuisine is very important. For this reason, the market stands burst with a variety of choices, from fresh ginger, leeks, and garlic to a huge assortment of dried spices.

COOKING TIPS

• When cooking the noodles, make sure to pay attention to the directions on the package: Asian noodles cook more quickly than Italian ones.
• You can find Chinese five-spice powder in the Asian section of supermarkets and in specialty shops.

SERVING TIPS

Serve litchees for dessert! Peel back the rough skin of fresh ones to reveal the fruit. Canned litchees are ready to eat.

 Hot cups of tea and, above all, rice wine should definitely not be left out.

SHANGHAI-STYLE NOODLES

CHINA

INGREDIENTS
(Serves 4)

- ¾ pound skinless boneless chicken breasts
- 1 pound bok choy
- 2 garlic cloves
- ½ pound Chinese egg noodles
- 1 tablespoon sesame seeds
- 3 tablespoons vegetable oil
- 2 tablespoons soy sauce
- 1 teaspoon cornstarch
- 1 teaspoon Asian sesame oil

INGREDIENT TIP

In this delicious stir-fry, you can use bok choy, Savoy cabbage, or Napa cabbage interchangeably.

Fine egg noodles, dressed up with tender chicken, Chinese bok choy, and sesame seeds, along with other seasonings, is a typical dish from the sprawling port city of Shanghai.

1 Rinse the chicken in cold water, pat dry, and cut into small chunks. Cut the bok choy in half and cut out the stem. Slice the leaves into thin strips. Peel and mince the garlic.

2 Cook the noodles in a large saucepan of boiling salted water according to the directions on the package. Drain in a colander and set aside.

3 Heat the wok over medium heat and stir-fry the sesame seeds until toasted. Transfer to a plate. Increase the heat to high, add the vegetable oil, and stir-fry the garlic for 30 seconds. Add the chicken and stir-fry until cooked through, 3–4 minutes. Add the bok choy and cook until tender yet crisp, 2–3 minutes.

4 In a cup, mix the soy sauce, cornstarch, and 2 tablespoons water; stir into the chicken mixture. Cook, stirring, until the sauce thickens, 1 minute.

5 Add the sesame oil and the noodles to the chicken mixture and stir-fry until heated through. Transfer to a platter and sprinkle with the sesame seeds.

Step 1

Step 4

Step 5

Preparation: 30 minutes
Cooking: 10 minutes
Per serving: 420 cal; 29 g pro; 15 g fat; 48 g carb.

TYPICALLY SHANGHAI
The port of Shanghai is known for its many fresh fish and seafood dishes. Yet chicken dishes, which are stewed, steamed, or stir-fried with various ingredients and spices, are equally popular there.

COOKING TIP

Asian sesame oil is pressed from toasted sesame seeds and has a strong nutty flavor—a little goes a long way. It can be found in Asian grocery stores or in the specialty-food section of most supermarkets. Because it is so strongly flavored, it is used as a seasoning, not for cooking.

SERVING TIPS

As an appetizer, try serving a warming chicken broth that's garnished with strips of fresh vegetables.

 Chinese beer or oolong tea strike a harmonious chord with this Asian dish.

INDONESIAN CHICKEN, PORK, AND SHRIMP STIR-FRY

INDONESIA

Fried egg noodles set the stage for this festive Indonesian favorite—called bami-goreng—which highlights chicken, pork, shrimp, and a chorus of vegetables.

INGREDIENTS
(Serves 4)

- ½ pound vermicelli
- 4 scallions
- ¼ head of Napa cabbage
- 1 fresh Thai bird or serrano chile
- 1 medium onion
- 1-inch piece fresh ginger
- 3 garlic cloves
- ½-pound piece pork loin
- 2 skinless boneless chicken breast halves
- ½ cup vegetable oil
- ¼ pound medium shrimp, shelled and deveined
- 2 tablespoons oyster sauce
- 2 tablespoons soy sauce
- 2 cups mung bean sprouts
- fresh cilantro sprigs

INGREDIENT TIP
You can substitute fish sauce for the oyster sauce—either is available at Asian markets.

1 Cook the noodles in boiling salted water according to the package directions, stirring often. Drain well in a colander.

2 Trim and thinly slice the scallions. Trim the cabbage and finely slice into strips. Trim and thinly slice the chile. Peel and finely chop the onion, ginger, and garlic. Cut the pork and chicken into thin strips.

Step 2

3 Heat a wok over high heat. Add ¼ cup of the oil and swirl to coat the pan. Add the noodles and cook, turning occasionally, until crisp. Transfer the noodles to a plate.

4 Pour the remaining ¼ cup oil into the wok. Add the chile, onion, ginger, and garlic; cook for 1 minute. Add the pork and chicken; stir-fry for 2 minutes. Add the shrimp and stir-fry for 2 minutes. Pour in the oyster sauce, soy sauce, and ½ cup of water. Add the cabbage and bean sprouts and cook, stirring often, for 2 minutes longer.

Step 3

5 Add the noodles; cook, tossing well, until heated through. Divide among 4 plates, then garnish with the scallions and cilantro.

Step 4

Preparation: 15 minutes
Cooking: 15 minutes
Per serving: 728 cal; 42 g pro;
38 g fat; 55 g carb.

TYPICALLY INDONESIAN
Bami-goreng is similar to nasi-goreng, a fried rice dish. On the island nation of Indonesia, consisting of more than 3,000 separate islands—among them Bali, Sumatra, and Java—nearly each region has its own distinctive version of these two dishes.

COOKING TIPS

• Fresh ginger can be kept for several months if peeled, placed in a clean glass jar, topped with either rice wine or sherry, covered securely with a lid, and refrigerated.

• If you don't have a wok, you can prepare this dish in a large, deep skillet.

SERVING TIPS

This dish is tasty served with rolled pancakes or shrimp chips, which are sold at Asian markets.

 Choose a refreshing white wine or jasmine tea as a suitable accompaniment.

KITCHEN GLOSSARY

This quick guide to ingredients and cooking terms will come in handy as you're preparing the pasta and noodle dishes in this book.

AL DENTE
Noodles cooked "al dente" should offer a slight resistance to the tooth—that is to say, they shouldn't be too soft. The cooking time will depend on the type of pasta that's used. Fresh noodles require less cooking time than dried varieties.

BALSAMIC VINEGAR
From the city of Modena, Italy, comes this especially refined, dark, pungent yet sweet vinegar made from white Trebbiano grape juice. Its reddish-brown color develops during the aging process.

FETA CHEESE
A young, crumbly, rindless cheese with a salty, tangy flavor. Originally from Greece, it's traditionally made with sheep's milk. Domestic varieties are sometimes made with cow or goat's milk.

OYSTER SAUCE
A dark-brown liquid made from oysters, brine, soy sauce, and sometimes other seasonings. Popular in Chinese cuisine, this seasoning sauce imparts a rich flavor.

PAPRIKA
A fine powdered spice made from a variety of sweet red pepper, its flavor ranges from mild and sweet to fiery. Hungarian paprika is considered the finest.

PARMESAN
Parmigiano-Reggiano, as this bold, firm Italian cheese is officially known, is made from cow's milk. It's often served freshly grated and can accompany most Italian pasta dishes.

PECORINO
This hard, aged sheep's-milk cheese has a rich, sharp taste. Though usually grated, some whittle shavings off to nibble with bread and wine. Among the varieties are Pecorino Romano and Pecorino Sardo.

OLIVE OIL
Olive oil is pressed from the fruit and seeds of the olive and is characterized by its hearty taste. Depending on the methods used in its production, it also varies greatly in color, quality, flavor, and cost.

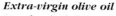

Extra-virgin olive oil
Unrefined oil obtained from the first pressing, it is not heated or treated with any chemical additives. Since it is carefully produced, it is of the highest quality and has superior flavor.

Virgin olive oil
An unrefined oil from the first pressing with an acidity level of 1–3 percent; extra-virgin's level is no more than 1 percent.

Olive oil
A combination of refined olive oil and virgin or extra-virgin olive oil.

Pasta Types

Asia and Italy are the two parts of the world where pasta has achieved the greatest culinary prominence. Here are some of the best-known varieties.

Asian noodles
Egg noodles
Made of wheat flour and eggs, these thin noodles come in dried bundles and are often added to soups or stir-fries.

Dried rice noodles
These extremely thin, translucent-white Chinese noodles are made from rice flour and can be deep-fried into a nest of crunchy strands or used in stir-fries and soups.

Italian pasta
Long, thin pasta
Capellini, linguine, spaghetti, and vermicelli are just some of the strands in this category. They're of varying thinness.

Stuffed pasta
Ravioli and tortellini are two examples of pasta pockets that have fillings of meat, cheese, or vegetables.

Long, flat pasta
Fettuccine, pappardelle, and tagliatelle are well-known examples of these ribbon pastas, which vary greatly in width.

Short, shaped pasta
Conchiglie (shells), farfalle (butterflies or bow ties), fusilli (corkscrews), penne (feathers), and rigatoni are a sampling of the shapes available.

Porcini
These Italian wild mushrooms have a strong, earthy flavor and are generally sold dried. Also grown in France, where they're called cèpes, they must be softened by soaking in water prior to use in sauces, ragus, and soups.

Ricotta
A light Italian cheese similar in texture to cottage cheese, ricotta is traditionally made from the whey of sheep's milk. Today it is also often produced from the whey of cow's milk.

Shiitake Mushrooms
Originally from Asia and now cultivated in America, the shiitake mushroom has a dark brown cap that averages 3-6 inches in diameter. Its meaty flesh has a full-bodied flavor.

Spaetzle
A German dish of tiny noodles or dumplings: Small pieces of dough are boiled, then used in soups or casseroles or tossed with butter and served as a side dish.

Pesto
An Italian sauce made from fresh basil, garlic, Parmesan, and pine nuts. Traditionally made with a mortar and pestle, pesto is particularly loved along the Ligurian coast where it originated.

Pine Nuts
Pine nuts are the seeds of several varieties of pine trees. In Italian cuisine, these small, rich, ivory-colored nuts are most commonly used in pesto but are also found in desserts. You can intensify their subtle flavor by roasting them in a dry pan.

ᴍ̲ᴇɴᴜ SUGGESTIONS

The following combinations should serve as inspiration to you when you want to surprise your family or friends with a multicourse meal that has an international flavor.

ITALY

FETTUCCINE IN A CREAMY CHEESE SAUCE P. 6
Marinated Artichoke Hearts
Lemon Tart
— ❖ —

TAGLIERINI WITH BOLOGNESE SAUCE P. 8
Shrimp Scampi Appetizer
Anise Biscotti
— ❖ —

SUMPTUOUS SALMON TAGLIATELLE P. 10
Grilled Vegetables
Oranges in Amaretto
— ❖ —

RAVIOLI WITH ZESTY CREAM SAUCE P. 12
Prosciutto, Tomato, and Mozzarella Salad
Poached Pears
— ❖ —

HERBED MUSHROOM PAPPARDELLE P. 14
Roasted Red Peppers
Cannoli
— ❖ —

PENNE ALL'ARRABBIATA P. 16
Cold Antipasti
Pistachio Ice Cream
— ❖ —

LINGUINI WITH RICOTTA AND HERBS P. 18
Tossed Greens
Coffee Mousse
— ❖ —

CREAMY TAGLIATELLE AND SPINACH P. 20
Fennel Salad
Chocolate-Dipped Strawberries
— ❖ —

FETTUCCINE WITH SICILIAN MEATBALLS P. 22
Fresh Pea Soup
Lime Granita
— ❖ —

CLASSIC ITALIAN PESTO FETTUCCINE P. 24
Seafood Salad
Watermelon Sorbet
— ❖ —

GREECE

SAVORY GREEK-STYLE RIGATONI P. 26
Baba Ganouj
Fresh Figs
— ❖ —

GERMANY

CARAMELIZED-ONION SPAETZLE P. 30
Cucumber Salad
Vanilla Bavarian
— ❖ —

SPINACH & MEAT-STUFFED NOODLES P. 32
Crisp Cabbage and Caraway Salad
Apple Compote
— ❖ —

FRANCE

ROAST DUCK OVER ORANGE NOODLES P. 34
*Endive Salad
with Creamy Dressing
Cherries Jubilee*

— ◆ —

HUNGARY

HUNGARIAN PAPRIKA NOODLES P. 36
*Beet Salad
Plum Cheesecake*

— ◆ —

USA

SPICY PENNE AND BROCCOLI P. 38
*Shrimp Cocktail
Chocolate Cream Pie*

— ◆ —

BOW TIES PRIMAVERA P. 40
*Squash Soup
Peach Cobbler*

— ◆ —

SPAGHETTI TETRAZZINI P. 42
*Wilted Salad with
Warm Bacon Dressing
Bread Pudding*

— ◆ —

AUSTRALIA

PROSCIUTTO PARMESAN PAPPARDELLE P. 44
*Tomato Soup
Apple Tart*

— ◆ —

SINGAPORE

SINGAPORE NOODLES AND SHRIMP P. 48
*Spring Rolls
Mango Mousse*

— ◆ —

JAPAN

NOODLES WITH SHIITAKE MUSHROOMS P. 50
*Salad with Miso Dressing
Sliced Fruit*

— ◆ —

CHINA

CRISPY NOODLE-AND-PORK STIR-FRY P. 52
*Sesame Shrimp Toasts
Pineapple Flambé*

— ◆ —

CASHEW SHRIMP VERMICELLI P. 54
*Clams in Black Bean Sauce
Watermelon*

— ◆ —

SHANGHAI-STYLE NOODLES P. 56
*Chinese BBQ Short Ribs
Orange Custard*

— ◆ —

INDONESIA

INDONESIAN CHICKEN, SHRIMP, AND PORK STIR-FRY P. 58
*Eggplant in Spicy Chili Sauce
Steamed Coconut Pudding*

— ◆ —

RECIPE INDEX

Photo Credits

Book cover and recipe photos:
©International Masters Publishers AB
Michael Brauner, Eising Food Photography, Dorothee Gödert, Neil Mersh, Peter Rees.

Agency photographs:
Introduction Comstock: page 4 upper left. Aigner: pages 4, 5 middle.
Lade: THF page 5 lower right. IFA: Kneer, page 5 upper right.
Photos for the 'Typically' sections: Aigner: page 10.
Bavaria: Schneiders, page 33.
Fotex: Stelzner, pages 52, 56.
IFA: Ebert, page 6; Putz, page 8; Amadeus, page 13; Diaf, page 24; Aigner, pages 14, 26;
     Ludwigs, page 36; Spence, page 38.
Image Bank: Curto, page 23; Heumader, page 30; Rossi, page 49; Jones, page 50; Chan, page 58.
Lade: Pictures, pages 17, 20; BAV, page 34; Krämer, page 46; Meissner, page 54; Rötzer, page 18.
Schapowalow: Neynaber, page 41. Zefa: McIntyre, page 42.

© MCMXCVIII International Masters Publishers AB.
Recipes of the World ™ IMP AB,
produced by IMP Inc. under license.
Printed in Italy.
ISBN 1-886614-81-4